WRANGLER, MY SPIRITUAL DIRECTOR DOG
   Author and Publisher
   Leighton S. Ford
   Charlotte, North Carolina

ISBN 978-0-9861463-9-8

Photography and artwork are by Leighton Ford unless indicated otherwise.

Printed by Lifetouch Services Inc.
Loves Park, Illinois
United States of America

©2015 Leighton S. Ford. All rights reserved.

Copyright ©2013 by Wendell Berry, from *This Day: Collected and New Sabbath Poems*.
Reprinted by permission of Centerpoint.

Copyright ©1998 by Wendell Berry from *A Timbered Choir*. Reprinted by permission of Centerpoint.

Printed on 10% PCW sustainable source certified paper using soy-based inks.

INTRODUCTION

When I leave home to drive to wherever I am going, my mind is often so preoccupied with what's ahead that I seldom consider how the familiar routes came to be.

The same could be said for the paths along which our lives and relationships with others move. We take for granted routines that daily, weekly, monthly wear grooves in our hearts, minds and souls.

I had just turned 73 when Wrangler, an Australian Cattle Dog, came into my life. Two years before, I had experienced within six weeks both a heart attack and prostate cancer. Fully recovered from both, I was pretty confident about my physical well-being.

But my lifework was changing. After 30 years of traveling to various events, young leaders I mentored were now coming to me for times of spiritual guidance. I was doing less speaking and more listening, writing and trying to slow my busy mind.

And, many longtime friends were retiring, moving away or showing the wear and tear of life.

I became more focused on an attentive life than a busy one — developing new "routes" for my life.

I needed a new friend for this new season. Then Wrangler arrived, a beloved companion for the decade to come.

He helped shape the contours of my "new" life, the habits of my heart. He became a large part of what spiritual teachers call the "rules of life" — ways in which we discern and practice God's presence. When I prayed, Wrangler usually was near. Only in looking back do I fully realize how much of life we shared together — hourly, daily, weekly. Wrangler was truly my "spiritual director dog." Spiritual director is a traditional term for a companion who points one toward the right path, to pay attention to God's direction.

Whether this book moves you to laughter or tears, my hope is that it is a reminder of how thankful we are to God for all of his gifts to us, including beloved pets whose unconditional love and loyalty has changed, even healed and saved, lives.

My hope is that that you and your dog share an unconditional love, that you are "with each other," one in heart and spirit.

Leighton S. Ford
2015

A CHRISTMAS GIFT

It was the week before Christmas 2004 when I found him, or, more truly, when we found each other.

Wrangler was a Christmas gift...to me...from me...and from God. And from Wrangler, too, for he gave himself to me.

I'm not sure how long I had been looking for him. It had been years since my wife, Jeanie, and I had a dog of our own. When this year I had put "dog" on my Christmas wish list, no one in the family thought I was serious.

But I was. A deep sense was growing within me that it was time to have a dog again, perhaps because I simply felt the need for another companion.

Where to look. I asked a good friend who decidedly suggested that I look for a rescue dog, not one from a puppy mill. And, she said she would help. So, I accepted her offer to do some scouting for me at the local animal shelter where she volunteered.

First, I went to see a lovely black dog named Lady. I liked her but didn't quite sense she was the one for me.

Then I got word there was another dog worth meeting, an Australian Cattle Dog. So with my grandson, Ben, I drove again to the shelter.

I SHOULD HAVE KNOWN RIGHT THEN THAT WRANGLER CAME TO TEACH ME TO PAY BETTER ATTENTION TO THE DAYS OF MY LIFE, THAT HE WAS GOING TO BE MORE THAN A PET…

We walked through the kennels where the sound of barking was nonstop, with dog after dog peering at us with longing eyes. I wanted to stop and talk to each one. We walked outside to the exercise yard, a very plain graveled area surrounded by metal fences, and waited.

The moment I saw Wrangler I was smitten. And perhaps he was, too. He sniffed a bit, then came over to where I was sitting. He moved very close to me. I rubbed his chin and ears. From that moment, we bonded.

"Gagi," said Ben, "I think this is your dog." He was right.

I knew nothing about Australian Cattle Dogs. I'd heard of Aussie shepherds but not Aussie Cattle Dogs. I had a lot to learn, but at that moment all I knew was that I wanted this dog.

"Where did he come from?" I asked my friend.

"We don't know. We think he may have been living in a barn. And, we have no idea why he was dropped here."

I knew. And I think he did, too.

"Does he have a name?"

"Wrangler, at least that's what's on his tag."

Wrangler, perfect name for an ACD. Aussie Cattle Dogs, also known as Heelers, come in several varieties. There are Red Heelers, known for their reddish coats, Queensland Heelers and Blue Heelers. Wrangler was the Blue variety, which is why to me he was Wrangler Blue Dog.

Australian Cattle Dogs are known to be exceptionally intelligent and industrious, and intensely loyal.

I love Australia and Australians. I have visited and spoken there many times across the years, more than any other country except Canada and the United States. Aussies have warm hearts and an adventurous spirit. They always gave me a good reception. Perhaps that's part of the reason I connected so quickly with Wrangler. My soul may be part Aussie.

I was taken immediately with Wrangler's appearance. He weighed about 50 pounds and a best guess was that he was about four or four-and-a-half years old. He had a thick and very soft coat of blue-black dark hair. Streaks of gray hair showed across his shoulder and back, almost as if he were prematurely gray. His legs and chest were highlighted with spots of light reddish tan.

A lovely gray-white streak came down from the crown of his head to his upper lip, and his pinkish tongue often stuck halfway out to the side like a canine imitation of basketball star Michael Jordan. At the other end, he sported a magnificent noble gray-white tail that he lifted high against his dark hair.

But what I noticed first, and what stays with me, were his eyes, soft brown with a tinge of blue, and steady. He could hold an attentive gaze like no creature I had ever seen, and stay focused for minutes or hours.

I should have known right then that Wrangler came to teach me to pay better attention to the days of my life, that he was going to be more than a pet, that he would be a companion, my spiritual director, a friend on life's journey, perhaps my best Christmas gift ever.

BRINGING WRANGLER HOME

I knew right away that day in the exercise yard that I wanted Wrangler. But I also knew I couldn't bring him home before Christmas with all the activities we had going on. And I wanted him to be a surprise. The problem was that he was up for adoption by the first person who wanted him. It was two days before Christmas and chances were that if I did not choose him someone else would.

So, what to do. I had to make a quick decision.

"Tell you what," said my friend, "if you do the adoption now, we'll keep him at our house until after the holiday, and you can get him then."

"Done," I said. Ben promised not to breathe a word about our visit to the shelter and we drove home smiling.

The Monday after Christmas I went to get my new friend. Wrangler hopped in the car. I learned instantly that he loved to ride and would go anywhere with anyone, anytime.

When we got to our house, no one was home. When Jeanie arrived home later, I met her at the door.

"Come here. I have something to show you," I said, and led her to the door of my home office.

She walked in, took a look at 50 pounds of blue-black hair and said, "What is that?"

That was Wrangler. "He's my Christmas gift to me," I said.

I haven't often been able to totally surprise my wife, but this time she was truly caught off guard.

"I can't believe you did this without telling me," she said.

"Because I knew none of you would give me what I said I wanted, a dog. So I am giving him to myself."

Jeanie loves animals. If she was piqued she didn't show it much, although she did say for awhile that she wished I had gotten a "pretty" dog, which I smugly reminded her every time someone said what a handsome dog he was and asked what kind he was, and I would proudly respond, "ACD, Aussie Cattle Dog, Blue Heeler and a rescue dog."

A RESCUE DOG

Jeanie quickly accepted and learned to love Wrangler.

I called him a rescue dog, but the truth is we rescued each other.

Why in the world anyone gave up this dog, so intelligent, so loyal, has always been a mystery to me. I think he was longing for a home and a person he could stay with always. Perhaps that's why he hardly ever took his eyes off me, unless he was chasing our cat.

Why were we drawn together? Perhaps because we both were adopted.

If I rescued him from his homelessness, he rescued me from a certain loneliness. Growing up, I was an adopted and only child, often very lonely, and never had a dog. The only pet I recall was a goldfish in a bowl. My one vivid memory of a dog is one who barked and scared me so badly on my way home from school that I ran to the porch of a strange house to feel safe. I wish I'd had a Wrangler then.

By the time we met, I was at a different place in my life. For years I had been very involved — overinvolved at times — in my work, speaking, often away from home for long periods, missing my family, leading projects and conferences, or when at home absorbed in research and writing. Now, in a shift of calling, most of my time was meeting one-on-one or with small groups of leaders I was mentoring. Many of the most significant partners in my former ministry lived in other places. Some, like my lifelong friend, Irv, who was always at my side, were getting older or passing on.

"You seem like a very lonely guy," someone had said to me in the middle of a busy conference. And I realized he was right. There was always lots to do. But my inner self was making me more aware of a "long loneliness" as Dorothy Day described her own life that had been covered in busyness. What I needed was not more passing acquaintances, but a close and constant friendship.

A WORKING DOG

I say that Wrangler rescued me, rescued me from being too serious and too preoccupied with busy-ness to enjoy each moment of each day.

Wrangler and I were alike in many ways. Wrangler was by nature a serious working dog. Play was a mystery to him. Often, on our walks, we met a huge, friendly neighboring Golden Retriever named Winston who would run in crazy circles around Wrangler and crouch in the classic "let's play" position. Wrangler would stare at him in puzzlement. When Winston picked up a branch and ran around waving it, Wrangler would watch for a bit, tentatively pick up a small stick for a minute or two, then drop it as if to say, "We're not here to play. We're here to work."

A WORKING DOG

I liked him, I admit without embarrassment,
not only with a pride of ownership
(or I should say partnership because
we don't "own" our dogs)
but because he was different.

"What kind of dog is that?"
I was often asked, and would explain,
while others would knowledgeably say,
"Blue Heeler, right?" and I would proudly answer,
"Right. Best dog there is."
"Is that a wolf?" children would ask
as we walked the schoolyard.

He was different. A working dog.
When we went for a walk he always
had to have something to carry,
a stick, a toy, anything
which he would drop after a few steps.
The neighbors laughed at his toys
scattered along the street.

Winston, a lovely large Golden
would come onto the schoolyard
so excited to see Wrangler he would
dash circles around him,
stick in mouth to play tug of war.
Wrangler would regard him
with a look of interest, if not disdain,
as if to say, "What are you doing?
We're not here to play. We're here to work."

LEARNING FROM MY BLUE DOG

He did not know much about play.
He knew a whole lot about love.

I loved him for his difference. And still do.

Life seems so complicated,
even at seventy-five.
I could learn a lot
from my Blue dog's life.
His needs are simple.
To be wanted.
To be fed.
To have his tummy rubbed.
To be allowed to bark at the birds
and dance in the water.
To be attended to.
To be with me.
What more should he want?
Or, for that matter, I?

July 24, 2007

WRANGLER MADE ME LAUGH MORE THAN I HAD IN YEARS.

In spite of his serious nature, Wrangler made me laugh more than I had in years.

I laughed when he played with his "jingle-bell doggie," a tiny brown musical dog. He would squeeze it and out would come "We Wish You a Merry Christmas." He would bite it over and over as we walked until the whole neighborhood reverberated with Christmas sounds. He squeezed it until it was worn out or lost. When spring arrived, I often came across bedraggled ones. Across the years, animal toy merchants may have ended the year in the black, profiting from repeated orders for Wrangler's doggie. I always kept two or three extras handy to replace when one was lost. Two are still on a shelf, unused.

The Christmas toy doggie made me laugh. But Wrangler's own favorite possession was a blue plastic bowl from which he ate for most of his years. When we headed out for a walk, he would invariably run back to his crate and pick up the bowl. He was a working dog after all, and needed to do his job. After a few steps, he would be drawn to sniff something and drop the bowl. The neighbors on our street got used to picking up the blue bowl and, with a knowing smile, dropping it off to its rightful owner. I still have that old blue bowl, still with a break in the rim.

Next to eating, Wrangler's favorite pastime was a water dance under the hose. He would spend most of his days in the backyard, regarding the birds, enjoying the sun, relaxing, waiting. All I had to do was pick up the green hose with the yellow sprinkler head and he was wide awake. He'd give two sharp barks, lift his tail, fix his gaze on my hand, and when I turned on the jet spray, he would attack it in full fury — dancing, whirling, running, grabbing, splashing, turning near cartwheels, leaping in the air, barking over and over. He was in full nonstop performance. When we had guests, they watched in amazement as he did his dance for them until the stream stopped and he stood shaking off the excess water, ready to take a bow. "I could have danced all night," as the song goes. Wrangler could have danced all day. He had other dances, too, but the water dance was his all-time bravo performance.

Wrangler also made me laugh when I saw him loping at full speed, his back half out of sync with his front half.

MR. SIDEWAYS

I told him I was going to rename him "Mr. Sideways."
My Australian Cattle Dog, that's him,
my Blue Heeler.
His lawful name is Wrangler.
Or, as I sometimes say, Tangler,
or simply WBD — Wrangler Blue Dog.

He's my buddy and
on this windy November afternoon
we're out together and
he goes ahead.
I have to laugh as I watch him,
back legs as bowed as any cowpoke,
loping along,
the front side of him seeming to go right
and the back side left
like a couple of freight cars
rolling from side to side.
That's why I call him "Mr. Sideways."
Or maybe it's because of the way
he sidled into my heart
when I rescued him
eight years ago.

He's getting on a bit now.
In the heat of summer
he's lazier, and slower.
But give him a cold afternoon like this!
His ears lift, his tail roves and he's off,
sniffing the neighborhood news,
barking off offending birds,
pretending the cars are cows to chase.

Because he's a good dog,
and only his bark is fierce,
I let him off his lead,
free to explore.
But no matter where he heads
he always stops, and looks back
to make sure
I'm still there.

October 2012

SIR B, WRANGLER'S NEMESIS

Wrangler made all of us laugh except Butternut, our cat of 14 years.

Our son found Butternut's mother, pregnant and lost, wandering a street in northern Virginia and ready to deliver a litter the next day. He chose one of the kittens and brought him to us. So, Butternut was also a rescue.

And he was regal. His golden hair and luxurious tail and disdainful demeanor were classic. Wrangler once tried to take a bite out of Butternut and he wound up with a mouthful of that golden hair.

Like most cats he was self-important, and was sure that he reigned not only over our house, but over the neighborhood. He was well known as the neighborhood cat. He would sit on a neighbor's stone fence for hours showing his disdain for dogs who stared and howled at him. At night, he prowled and on cold nights found places where he could stay warm, although we never discovered exactly where.

"Sir B" was a hunter, the scourge of any creature who dared show up in our backyard and dared him to catch them, which he so often did, leaving his prey at the back door to let us know he liked us.

I CALLED HIM "SIR B" FOR THERE WAS SOMETHING REGAL ABOUT HIM.

If Wrangler was my dog, Butternut was Jeanie's cat. Jeanie came to love Wrangler, too, but Butternut was hers. His routines were simple. When feeding time came, Sir B showed up exactly on time. In the morning he ate his breakfast, then leaped onto Jeanie's bed, knocked away the paper she was reading and stroked her in masculine contentment. While we ate, he lay on the table eyeing my plate, hoping to share a bite.

During the day, Butternut explored or sat in the sun. In the evening, he snuggled next to Jeanie as we watched TV or on her bed as she read, until he saw me coming. He would leap to the floor ready to disappear into the dark for his evening visit to the corners of his kingdom.

Our home was his territory. He had a deep dislike for strangers who dared to come, except for family and one or two friends.

So, five years into his reign, when Wrangler arrived, they both became very serious — serious foes. Sir B glared from (usually) safe distances at this dark presence that invaded his "castle" and sovereign territory. They had more than one scuffle and never reconciled.

BUTTERNUT'S NIGHTMARE COME TRUE

After reading Jane Kenyon's "The Blue Bowl" on burying the cat.

Butternut — that is his given, if not legal name —
son of Callie.
I call him Sir B for there is something regal about him.
For several years he had the run of the house,
his mansion, his estate,
showing only a disdaining annoyance
when aliens invaded
and he would depart.

Until Wrangler (aka WBD) came, a disturbing presence.

The late Cocoa was thoroughly cowed by Sir B,
unable to look the cat straight in the eye,
always averting his gaze.

Not WBD, who stares, unblinkingly,
with a teleological curiosity,
always wanting to edge closer but
far enough to evade the claws
of this prince of the house.

Down the street, Sir B will sit
for hours on
a neighbor's stone fence,
eyes closed,
knowing full well that his being there
infuriates their resident house dog,
who will yip at the window
for hours on end,
Sir B remaining totally unmoved.

But now! He has to live cautiously,
be sure the dark invader is not on the porch
when he ventures out,
or from across the street
wait anxiously
until sure the yard is clear.

A dark figure has come to hound
his lordship's dreams.

October 15, 2006

WRANGLER'S MANY NAMES

What Sir B called him under his breath I would not care to guess, but Wrangler, his name when we met, was a perfect name for an Australian Cattle Dog, who was as bow-legged as any cowboy, and would have loved nothing more than to herd cows. Where we lived that was not possible, so he had to be content with barking at passing cars.

Sometimes I called him WBD for Wrangler Blue Dog so perfectly matching his lovely dark blue shape, blue-gray tail and spots of tan under his chin. Other times Wrangler became "Tangler," wrapping his lead around and around me.

He was "Mr. Green Eyes" when he came from the garage to meet us as we arrived home at night, those penetrating eyes shining in the headlights.

But for me, he was, is and always will be mostly "Wrangli."

Even now when out walking, perhaps late at night by myself, I hear myself calling into the night air, "Wrangli, come boy. I'm waiting." I see his ears perk up and he is on his way.

"There's only one dog that is a lifetime dog," says my friend, Elizabeth, who introduced me and Wrangler years ago. "Wrangler is yours."

Wrangler was my lifetime dog, not only making up for my dogless boyhood, but also sharing every day of these latter years.

I think we understood each other almost like brothers, or great friends. He read my emotions and my inclinations, at least he learned to interpret them. When my longtime ministry partner, Irv, was very ill, I was thinking how I would miss him. Wrangler sensed my sadness, came over, put his head against my leg. He understood.

For nine years we did almost everything together. When I wrote or watched TV or read, he sat by my side, watching, waiting, ready for me to move, his ears perking up at the slightest motion, instantly ready for a walk or a ride. He was so loyal, so intelligent and so attached.

His only fault (as poet Billy Collins wrote of his dog) was that he must have thought I was God. In reality, he helped me focus on God.

MONOPHONIC CATTLE DOG

Wrangler is a very expressive creature
but not in sounds.
He has a limited vocabulary — "WHARK"
Which is a variation on BARK because his is:

Loud
Sharp
Short
Fierce
Insistent

I know (Don't ask me how; I just do.)
that he has poly-feelings
(love, happiness, excitement, frustration)
but a monotone.

So I have had to learn to interpret WHARK!!
which variously means

Rub my tummy!
Food time!
Garbage truck (a cow look-alike) passing by.
The mailman!
Stop talking to these other people.
Pay attention to me.
You've been writing (reading) long enough; let's walk.
C'mon, keep moving.

Oh, yes, and there is one other sound.
A brief, low, resigned moan when his
WHARKS get no response.

I wonder sometimes if he gets frustrated
with his limited vocabulary.
But he does have other communication skills.

His body language is quite expressive.
His tail of welcome ("Oh boy, you came back.")
And, oh yes,
his eyes say it all.

July 2013

WRANGLER AND "RED RIBBONS"

As Wrangler and I took our usual Sunday walk in the woods he began to dash back and forth, barking at a flock of small red birds. They flew from tree to tree partly in fright but also teasing the black creature that was upsetting their quiet Sunday morning.

In the evening, we took a final walk of the day, Wrangler off his lead. After several minutes, I could not see him; he was so dark in the dimness around. I called and whistled, and finally saw his Blue Heeler shape across the street, running in circles.

This time it was not red birds flying in the trees but red ribbons fluttering above our neighbor's wall in the glow of a lamp. Wrangler was barking furiously, jumping as high as he could, trying to climb the wall, determined to catch those red things flapping noisily in the breeze.

I stepped back and watched him run and hoot, leap and fall back, all his dog instincts at work, determined to catch those flapping ribbons that were so frustratingly out of reach. Did he think they were the birds from the morning tormenting him again? It was serious business to him, but so comical to me that I bent over in laughter.

In church this particular Sunday, we sang praise with the "citizens of heaven." I wonder if some of the angels were smiling, expecting red birds and Blue Heelers in heaven.

THE LOVE OF GOD, THE LOVE OF A DOG

The Bible tells us that God's lovingkindness is steadfast. His is not an "if" love — *if* we are good enough, *if* we care enough, *if* we are kind enough. It is not a "because" love — *because* we deserve it, which often we do not. It is an "in spite of" love, *in spite of* how often we fall short. God's love is unconditional, a love for all seasons and beyond all reasons.

Often, it's hard for us to feel worthy of such a love, to accept it and certainly to comprehend it.

Perhaps that's why God gave us dogs, and why he sent Wrangler to me. Whatever I was doing, whatever my mood, Wrangler was there, "with me," to love me unconditionally.

"A friend loves at all times..." wrote the great king, Solomon (Proverbs 17:17).

Through the faithful devotion of my doggie friend, God gave me a glimpse of his steadfast and unchanging love.

Through God's *in spite of* love and his amazing grace, may we love him, others and ourselves as he first loved us.

Lifetouch Image

WRANGLER TAUGHT ME TO PAY ATTENTION

Poets, says Mary Oliver, know how to pay attention. Wrangler must have been something of a poet, for he was a model of attentiveness.

When we went for walks in the schoolyard, and I stopped to talk to friends, Wrangler would sit perfectly still (for awhile), his eyes fixed unwaveringly on me. My neighbor, Todd, would often shake his head in amazement and say, "I never saw a dog who could be so fixated on one person, and never waver for a moment."

Then, after awhile, Wrangler would give a sharp bark as if to say, "Come on, this is my time with you. You can talk to friends other times. Let's walk."

So, if Wrangler taught me to laugh, he also gave me lessons in paying attention. Because of my often overly busy mind, I needed to learn to pay attention. Next to Jeanie, Wrangler was my best tutor. The way he paid attention to me taught me to keep my inner gaze on God, my heart alert to his signals.

I think God sent Wrangler to me in part to help me be more attentive both to what is going on around and inside me, and to remind me that a working dog and a busy writer/preacher both need still times in a changing world.

MY SPIRITUAL DIRECTOR DOG

I thought of Wrangler as many things — a Blue Heeler, a curious and always hungry dog, a great buddy, but never as a spiritual director, that is until one Sunday.

It had been a very cold night so I let Wrangler sleep indoors. When I woke and was saying a morning prayer, he got as close to me as he could, then went to eat.

I continued a time of reflection, reading an article on the practice of contemplative prayer, and how in prayer we spend time in silence with God who longs to spend that time with us.

Then it was time for a walk. Wrangler was usually so eager to bound out but this particular morning he was keeping in very close step with me. We had been going to dog training (which is really "mister" training) and together learning that when I said "with me" he was to stay by me and not strain ahead. He was so strong and eager that it was not easy for him to learn. But this day that's exactly what he was doing. When we got to a favorite woodsy area and rested near a bridge in the sun he sat as close to me as he could, and put his head on my lap.

Wrangler wanted to be "with me," to be together in the sun and quiet of that cold Sunday morning. When we walked, I didn't have to hold him back. When I sat, he sat. There were no words at first, just the warm feeling of each other's company and that we belonged together.

As Wrangler and I rested, I said over and over, "Be still and know that I am God." Wrangler listened attentively to my voice.

And that's when I realized Wrangler Blue Dog had been my spiritual director, at least for the day. He did not tell me what I had to do. He just showed me by his actions, without a word. It was as if the Lord had told him, "Wrangler, show that friend of yours that he doesn't have to make some great effort, practice some heroic discipline. All he has to do is be with me, and soak in my Word and my Presence, that I just want him to stay with me."

Wrangler was not listed on any Web site of available spiritual directors. But perhaps he should have been.

P.S. I have to report that one time Wrangler tried to eat Butternut, and ended up with a mouthful of golden hair. Even spiritual directors can backslide.

WRANGLER LOST IN THOUGHT

What do you think about,
doggie of mine,
lying there on your throw,
nose between your front paws
like some graying philosopher,
a canny canine muse?
Are you puzzling out the
mysteries of your universe?
Or just waiting for the day
to unfold?
Do you daydream
about birds and rabbits?
Ask yourself why we come to
the mountains and if
there is a pattern?
Do you wonder, ever,
why I brought you home?
Ever remember
where you were before,
or the people who treated
(or mistreated) you?
When you turn your head
what are you listening for?
And when your unblinking eyes
stare ahead do you ask yourself
what you are waiting for?
When I read, are you curious
about what I am looking at?
When I pray,
do you wonder who is there,
besides you,
who I am talking to?

May 21, 2008, after reading from Psalm 62, "My soul, wait in silence..."

MORNINGS

Each morning Wrangler would be waiting for me by the door to the garage. When I opened the door, he would stand, stretch into his "down dog" posture with an upward "oooppp" and happily go to eat from his famous blue bowl, then quickly move to the backyard to view life from the porch or, on cold days, find a spot in the sun.

For years we took an early trek through our neighbor's yard, and crossed the street into a private park with a creek running through, along with frequent pauses for him to sniff "the morning news."

He almost made news himself one morning, nearly causing me to have a heart attack! I saw him step across a wriggling shape on the path and realized he'd had a close encounter with a small copperhead.

Nearly every Sunday morning for years, I'd take along Wendell Berry's book of Sabbath poems and sit on a little wooden bridge that crossed the creek. Wrangler would nose around, take a quick drink, then come and roll over to have his tummy rubbed while I read and prayed.

Weekday mornings, I would be at my computer. Wrangler sat quietly by my side until he thought I'd done enough. Then he would interrupt my writing with a sharp bark to announce that I (and he) needed to walk. If I stood, his tail would wag joyfully. If I ignored him, he would give a disgusted grunt and sit back for awhile.

Saturday mornings, I often rode my bike in the deserted schoolyard, while Wrangler ran beside me, sometimes nipping at my calf as if I was a disobedient cow, then running off to explore. He might wander away for a few minutes, but I knew he would always make sure I was still in sight, and when he spotted me, race back.

MORNING WALK WITH THE WOODPECKERS

On our morning walk
in the water places,
Wrangler and I heard the
brrrrrrrrr-rat-a-tat-tat
of two woodpeckers,
one close and low,
one far and high,
picking up their takeout breakfast
from some flyby trees.

It was a welcome sound.

Most days now we hear
the grunting and groaning
of earthmoving machines
leveling the ground for
one overgrown house-to-be, and
at the insistence of the new owners,
felling every tree.

So we were grateful,
Wrangler and the woodpeckers and I,
for each tall still standing tree.

April 5, 2009

AFTERNOONS

There's a *New Yorker* cartoon of a dog sitting on a sofa in his psychiatrist's office. The good doctor, puffing on his pipe, pen in hand, says "Now tell me more about this imaginary fence."

I showed the cartoon to Wrangler but he didn't get it. He did know there was an invisible something in the yard that kept him contained but also allowed him to roam off-leash. (He did break through it twice, both times spotting and chasing Sir B who was sitting just beyond the invisible fence, gloating.)

Somehow, whenever I returned from an afternoon appointment, Wrangler knew the instant I drove into the driveway and ran immediately to greet me, with a wag of the tail and his eyes inviting me to join him for a walk.

SNIFFING THE DAY

Yesterday my dog and I
walked the Greenway,
or, more exactly,
walked and stopped.
Every few feet he had to sniff.
Impatiently, I pulled him on,
lost in my thoughts,
sniffing my memories.

On the way back the slanting sun
cast our shadows ahead,
a tall one, a short one,
and, in my mind, missing ones.

Wrangler kept pulling away
and I pulled him on,
until, in a moment,
I gave in, thinking,
"Why not let him sniff?
He needs this moment
of pleasure, and would it
not be good to find joy
simply in sniffing the day?"

January 24, 2013

We had our favorite places, sometimes on the Springs Greenway where he would casually gaze at the sheep and goats, sometimes in the local doggie park where he would sniff disinterestedly at a few visiting dogs. Wrangler was not one to socialize with his own kind. While they chased each other, he would be scouting spots interesting to him.

I could name half a dozen other favorite spots — including an outdoor classroom for a nearby school where we would stop and converse awhile — places in nature which became places of the heart, trails I know I would never have found if not for our walks together.

EVENINGS

Wrangler liked soft places to sit while we watched TV in the evenings. Usually he'd stay close. But if he disappeared, we knew where to find him — on Jeanie's nice living room sofa or on my bed.

There was one problem. He was a shedder. His lovely thick blue-black hair was soft and plenteous. When I brushed him with the FURminator, it came out in great rolls and clumps. But it also came out by itself with no brushing at all.

More than once, the cleaning woman would be sure to show Jeanie how the spread on my bed was loaded with signs of his presence.

We tried our best to keep him on a throw where loose hair didn't matter. But we couldn't always keep him off the soft places. And, I confess, I didn't want to.

His hair might have been a bother. It also made him beautiful.

Wrangler knew exactly when it was bedtime. He would come for his last walk of the day and his nightly treat. Ears would lift, tail begin to twitch at my slightest move.

I had to watch him carefully on dark nights. With his dark shape, he could easily disappear among bushes or shrubs. Once, when he was newly with us, he slipped through the schoolyard gate which had been left ajar. I was in near panic for long minutes, unable to locate him until he happily came trotting back to me.

Most of the time, though, he stayed close, especially on cold, clear winter nights when we watched the stars above.

UNDER THE MYSTERY

Under this April evening sky
I stand in the schoolyard
with my Blue dog
who noses around the aroma of earth
while I look for awhile at
the crescent moon,
the far thrown stars,
and the vast reaches beyond,
thinking of the mystery
of it and that I want
to understand it.
But then I think, no.
That's not what I want.
Not to understand the mystery.
But to stand before it.

April 9, 2008

AN EVENING WALK

Wrangler stops to sniff,
I breathe the sweet almost summer wind,
a raindrop strokes my face,
the clouds give promises of more.
For a moment now
troubles seem so far away.

June 9, 2010

ONE WARMHEARTED OLDER GUARD WOULD STOP, ROLL DOWN HIS WINDOW AND LET WRANGLER JUMP IN THE FRONT SEAT. THEY WOULD RIDE TO THE END OF THE STREET AND BACK, WRANGLER SITTING IN REGAL SPLENDOR.

Sometimes Wrangler and I played games. "Stay," I would tell him, walking backward away from him. And he stayed, until at "come" he would come racing for a quick hug.

One "state secret" I can now reveal for the first time. Wrangler's number one favorite thing (next to eating and water dances) were his occasional nighttime rides with one of the security guards making his rounds on our street. Wrangler would see the white car coming and be on full alert. One warmhearted older guard would stop, roll down his window and (if no one was watching) let Wrangler jump in the front seat. They would ride to the end of the street and back, Wrangler sitting in regal splendor.

Someone must have reported this because the guard regretfully had to inform me he shouldn't give rides anymore. Wrangler never did understand. He continued to watch for the security car, expecting his ride to show up, and turned away with disappointment when he was not invited to ride.

ECLIPSED

My Blue dog and I sat outside
a long time the other night
during the eclipse of the moon.
I, fascinated by the colors, watched
the glowing red magically turn
molten yellow and
into a deep mottled mauve.
He, showing no inclination
either to gaze or
bay at the moon, was
content to sit by my side
and have his ears rubbed.
I imagine he was puzzled:
why were we sitting outside
on the back steps of the porch
for half an hour in the dark
saying nothing?
I am pretty sure by now he
understands that, like most humans,
his mister is capable of the most
bizarre and unexpected fits,
so his job was to
provide some balance and constancy
while the moon and I changed.
Even if I was moonstruck
for awhile, he was letting me know
I was going to be ok,
and when I came back to earth
and normalcy
he would still be there.

February 23, 2008

A CONVERSATION AT BEDTIME

"C'mon, jump up here. There you go. That's a little harder now, isn't it?"
　"A little."
"What are you staring at?"
　"You. Tell me something."
"You're handsome. I love your soft dark hair and your long gray tail."
　"Tell me more."
"And those brown and white spots on your neck."
　"Tell me something else."
"And the way you look at me with those brown eyes. You never blink. You're uncanny."
　"Tell me more."
"I don't know why anyone ever gave you up."
　"Tell me more."
"I love you."
　"Can I stay here? I like soft places. I won't tell."
"Sure. You can stay next to me tonight."
　"Mmmmm."

DAYS AT THE LAKE

About an hour north of Charlotte, friends have a condominium on Lake Norman which they make available to me or others for personal retreats.

Every few weeks I would make a foray there to get away from routine responsibilities, to think, pray, to write. Always, Wrangler came along, excited for an early morning ride. I'd stop for breakfast. Then, when we arrived, if the weather was good, we'd sit outside by the lake, he by my side, sniffing the water's edge, watching the waves, the clouds together.

In the afternoons we would take a long walk to the end of the lakeside road, breathing in fresh air, wandering down to the sandy beach.

An introvert by nature, while I love good company, I need times away from others. During these times, Wrangler was just the company I needed — an introvert like me, not terribly social, patient, content just to be with me as I was with him.

We could be together and know that God is God, the God of all creatures, the God who brought us together.

BY THE LAKE

...I am here, in this solitude, before you,
and I am glad because you see me here.
For it is here, I think, that you want to see me
and I am seen by you.
                              Thomas Merton

I sit for a long while, doing nothing,
only looking, listening
Blue dog by my side.
I am the only thing still.
The long curving waves change direction constantly
at the shifting nudges of the February breeze.
A dazzle of crystal light shapes
like a flight of brilliant birds
glint and go and come again.
Light and dark swatches on the surface
are dance partners switching places constantly
in some random rhythm of their own.

Reflected trees and grasses stretch outward
as sharp as Ansel Adams photographs,
then break and fade in troubled water.
On the sky marshmallow clouds
are painted, puffed immobiles
until high winds thin them
into toffee pulls above the far horizon.
At my feet Wrangler dozes in the sun,
rises, barks, walks restlessly
to sniff the rocks and then returns.
A long-billed dark white-throated duck
surfaces from who knows where,
swivels his head curiously from side to side,
dives below for twenty seconds only to
appear again fifty feet away.

I only sit here, still,
alone.

Until I say, "I am here."

And One answers,
"I see you. Welcome."

Lake Norman, *February 8, 2006*

A CONVERSATION IN SUMMER

We took Wrangler with us when we went to visit Jeanie's brother. After the visit, he was depressed for a full day.

"You look so sad."
"I am. Billy's nice. But I don't like his three dogs."
"Why?"
"You left me outside. I came to find you. They cornered me, all three. I just stood there. They stared at me. I was so scared. I couldn't move. You left me tied by those bushes by Billy's office. It thundered. And those nasty yellow bugs got into my hair and stung me. I was half-crazy. Please don't take me there again."
"Okay."
"I don't feel like talking anymore. Just let me be alone."

JULY 4TH ENDING

Wrangler and I
waited out
the fireworks
and the storm
last night,
he head down
between his paws
to muffle the sharp
exchanges.
I trying to read
at last put down my book
wanting only to discern
beyond the clamor
the voice of someone
miles away until
my eyes grew heavy
and I slept.

July 4, 2013

NOT A HAPPY DOGGIE

On a morning in February, Wrangler and I were returning from our morning walk. As we walked through a neighbor's yard, I suddenly saw their dog running at us.

In a second the dog and Wrangler were at it, growling, circling, snapping.

Not until we got home did I see the red stains on the side of Wrangler's leg, finding a wide gash which required 25 staples to close the wound, and making it necessary for him to wear a collar to keep him from licking and pulling at the staples.

Wearing his collar, drooping his head, he personified the "hangdog" look for weeks.

After the collar came off, he was close to being our happy dog again. But I could tell he was showing signs of getting older, much as I wanted to deny it.

STAINS ON THE CARPET

The blood stains on my carpet
are from my dog
gashed in an attack
by another dog, across the street.
I wonder how much blood
has seeped from my soul's
wounds across the years
and from the souls and bodies
of all creatures in this world,
and is ours as precious to You
and as painful
as his to me
and Yours to us?

February 7, 2013

A CONVERSATION IN WINTER

Wrangler came to me in winter. I remember him on winter nights, snoozing by our fireplace, begging to sleep next to me instead of in his crate. But especially I remember one winter when an unusually heavy snow blanketed our North Carolina home.

He had been in one of his rare fights with another dog, and had to have several staples in his leg to help him heal. He had to wear one of those ungainly E-Collars, similiar to those Elizabethan queens wore, to keep him from pulling out the staples.

He looked so woebegone that I asked him one morning, "How are you?"

"Miserable," he said, "I hate wearing this thing."

"Sometimes it helps to write your feelings," I said. "Why don't you write something?"

Can you believe what he came up with?

SNOW DOG

Today I am one free dog.
Hallelujah!
For two weeks now
I've had to wear this weird cone
on my head
that makes me look like a creature
from outer space.

I got attacked by another dog
Who tore a big hole in my hip.

They put twenty staples in me to fix it.
Can you imagine? The embarrassment?
Being a stapled dog?

But the worst was having to wear
this space helmet-like thing.
Not just that it made me ugly
but what a nuisance.
It made me bump into doors
and furniture and my mister's leg
trying to find my way.

If I were not such a good-natured
Christian dog I would have growled,
"Take this (expletive deleted) thing off.
It's making me depressed."

But then I found a use for it!
We had snow — two inches of it —
and this contraption turned out to be
the best scoop you can imagine!
I scooped up heaps of that
wonderful, cool stuff,
half filled my cone with it.

So today, when they took the staples out,
I wanted to tell the vet tech,
"Lady, you made me look like an astro-dog
wearing that E-Collar thing.
But I got the best of you and it.
When I scooped up all that snow
my mister said I looked like
the most delicious ice cream cone
he'd ever seen!"

So, hallelujah!
From one free and happy dog.

Wrangler Ford, *February 2013*

A CONVERSATION IN THE MOUNTAINS

Each fall I meet with one of our mentoring groups, the Sigdors, at a house in the mountains. Wrangler always came along.

"Whew, my joints are tired. We must have walked five miles today. When do we eat?"

"Yes, uphill a lot, too. Do you like the big guy?"

"He's okay, for an Anglican priest. He talks funny though. And he could lose some weight. But I like him. When do we eat?"

"You like them all?"

"Sure. They treat me like one of them. They let me join the circle when they join hands and talk to God. I like to hear them talk and laugh. Sometimes, though, they...well, they get sad. I come close to them then, roll over for them to scratch my tummy and make them laugh.

"Hey, are you listening? When do we eat?"

"They say you're an honorary Sigdor."

"I'll make them honorary dogs. Maybe they'll even let me puff one of those things they smoke around the fire."

"So, do you really want a cigar?"

(Pause)

"Maybe to sniff, but I'd rather have a biscuit."

A CONVERSATION ON SANDY'S PATH

On one of our walks, I took Wrangler to the path that runs along a creek behind Myers Park High School. Our son, Sandy, had been a cross-country runner, and often ran on this very path. But he had a heart arrhythmia problem called WPW syndrome, which when it kicked off made his heart beat at a life-threatening rate. He had two surgeries to correct the problem, but did not survive the second. His classmates placed a bench and a plaque along this creek in his memory. Sandy was given a wonderful Golden Retriever after his first surgery. Czar was hit and killed by a car two years to the week after Sandy died. Sandy would have loved Wrangler.

"Where are we going?"

"Down this path, where Sandy used to run."

"Sandy was a runner?"

"A good one. He ran the mile and cross-country and he ran right here."

"Was he fast...as fast as me?"

"He was fast, but you might be faster."

"Did he win races?"

"Quite a few. Once he was running a mile. He was way ahead. Then he fell. He got up and ran and fell again. Then he crawled across the finish line and won."

"What's this plaque say?"

"That he was president of his class...that he was a runner...that he finished his race."

"I wish I knew him."

"You will, and his doggie, Czar. You will like them, and they'll like you."

"And we'll all have a long run...and never get tired."

A WALK ON HIS FIFTIETH BIRTHDAY

For Sandy

Wrangler and I, down
a path of shadowed leaves, fallen,
to a wooden bench, well-worn,
near a half-hidden plaque,
only slightly marred,
by a stream whose memories
have never stopped running.
We sit awhile and listen.
I talk about him.
We leave, the treetops
high above incandescent
in a late afternoon glory.

November 14, 2010

NOVEMBER 27, 1981

This is the day our son died.

It's not hard to remember.
Outside, early,
a red bird rests on the feeder.
The sky is cloudy.
A few brown leaves fall singly.

Wrangler my Blue dog
chews on his mat until
he understands, wise friend,
and comes to sit by me, quietly
asking for nothing.

I allow myself to recognize again
the returning scent of pain
like a smoky candle
which has not quite gone out.

November 27, 2011

GOODBYE TO SIR B

Butternut was beginning to show his age. He had been a hunting cat his whole life, the scourge of other animals in our backyard. But the morning offerings of a fated bird, squirrel or rabbit had stopped showing up on our back porch for quite awhile.

Sir B also was spending much more time lying in the sun on the stone wall of our patio.

Our cat had a very "un-cat-like" practice of following Jeanie and me when we went for a Sunday afternoon walk in the schoolyard. He would pause often and scan the field to make sure no dogs were around, and then catch up and walk sedately behind us. It seemed a dog-like practice for a cat.

Sir B began to lose weight and limp. Jeanie sensed something was wrong. Then we found a deep oozing of blood in his front paw. We put ointment on it and waited, but it kept bleeding.

On an October morning we put him in his carry box, Sir B resisting as always, clawing and pushing his head out. He hated that box. We took him to the vet who confirmed our fears. It was a cancer. He could operate, but advised against it.

The next day, our grandson went with me as we put our beautiful cat of 15 years on the table at the vet's to say goodbye. Sir B lay there quietly, clearly sensing something important was happening. We stroked him, thanked him. He was given an injection to make him calm and sleepy. I gave him a final loving pat and walked out. There was no way I could stay for the final dose.

FOR BUTTERNUT...
AKA SIR B

Something is missing in our house today,
a prowling feline presence
who came to us fourteen years ago
and staked a claim to his territory,
which extended to only God knows where.
We never knew where he spent his nights,
only that every morning he was sure to turn up
for breakfast, tail raised in regal, golden splendor,
which is why I nicknamed him Sir B.

Our grandson and his father brought him to us
one Christmas on a long drive from Virginia,
he riding most of the way on the dashboard of their car.

On Thursday that same grandson rode with me
on the very short drive to the vet
where Sir B was very quiet, lying low on a padded table,
not at all the personage
who hunted at night and proudly offered his
latest catch to us in the morning.

The vet folk were very kind and gentle.
They left us with him for awhile, to stroke
and whisper our care, and a prayer.
Then they did what they needed to do.
He became sleepy.
We left.

Wrangler, our Blue Heeler, doesn't realize he's gone.
The two of them declared a war
from the time Wrangler invaded Sir B's sovereign turf,
and never came to a truce.

Butternut was smaller, but faster.
Wary of an attack he could streak
like a golden arrow across the street to safety.

He was also canny,
knowing exactly the line of the invisible fence
beyond which his foe would not pass,
and where he could lie in smug disdain.

Yet he had one dog-like trait.
The neighbors marveled, and so did we
that when we went for a walk in the schoolyard
Butternut would tag along.

Last Sunday we took a different path
through a neighbor's yard, down their driveway
to the woods and by a stream.
We were surprised when he followed us there,
trotting behind, catching up
in spite of an open, bleeding wound
(a sign on his paw of other creeping ills
which could not be fixed).

He had never walked that route with us before
(although Wrangler had, many times).
I wonder, smart intuitive cat that he was, whether
he knew it was time to take a final jaunt,
perhaps to show us his nighttime haunts,
or, even better, to go where Wrangler had gone,
a preview of that coming age and space
where they and we and all God's creatures
made new will finally walk together.

October 26, 2013

WRANGLER SLOWS DOWN

He had not been able to jump onto my bed at night for quite awhile. When we went for a drive, instead of leaping easily into the back of the SUV, he needed a helping hand.

When we walked through the woods or down by a creek, Wrangler was much more careful, gingerly feeling with a paw before he went down by the creek for a drink, starting down a slope carefully, then turning back. His night vision also seemed to confuse him. When we went out for our evening walks he often stood a bit unsure of where to go.

He dozed more in the sun. Jeanie also noted that his hearing was lacking a bit. She had to call him several times to come from his spot in the backyard when it was time for his supper. It was most unusual for the dog who before could outrun any sprinter when it was time to eat.

Yet, his water dances were as acrobatic as ever. And he could still rush furiously at flocks of geese that landed in the schoolyard.

But he was nearing 14 and he was even more possessive of me as he grew older. He would become impatient if I stopped to talk to anyone while we were out walking. A sharp bark would remind me, "This is my time, my walk. Forget about them. Let's get going."

He wanted more of me. He didn't like me to go off without him, and he couldn't wait until I got back.

FATHER'S DAY EVENING

We sit outside, Wrangler and I,
just off the porch,
sharing a slice of lemon pound cake.
It feels so good, just to be here in the quiet,
except for the humming squads of summer.

Weary from a morning full of speaking,
an afternoon of lovely family talk,
I need time alone, the only company
my dog, flashing fireflies,
and Mary Oliver's poems.

Final crumbs discovered and devoured,
Wrangler retires to his favorite corner
where, still and always hungry, he chews his mat.
"Come here," I call,
"Let me read a poem about a dog."

He pretends not to hear; I call again.

Reluctantly he stretches and comes,
with enough hesitation
to make me wonder if his sight is failing
or whether he too is tired at the end of day.
"Here's a poem about a dog. Percy.
Percy didn't like books. He ate one just one time."

I don't think Wrangler likes them either.
Not impressed with Percy or poetry
he rolls to have his belly rubbed,
back leg joining vigorously
in this tribal ritual.

"Wrangler," I breathe,
"please don't get older, please,"
sensing a hint of tears,
not of disappointment,
but out of deep love, and thinking
how fast a day goes by.

With no introduction, or invitation,
something large, a shadow,
or shadow of a shadow
a whirring blur, beats the air
and sits, staring, suspiciously
on the dark limb of a tree.

I approach.
The stranger waits,
and then, owl or
something otherwise,
without a sound is gone
into the dimness.

June 17, 2012

ANOTHER NIGHT BEFORE CHRISTMAS

It was Christmastime nine years ago when I found Wrangler, and he found me.

And it was a night two weeks before Christmas when he left.

With his unwavering gaze, Wrangler took in everything.

But this night, those eyes betrayed him.

I have replayed it over and over, like a movie in very slow motion.

We came home late from dinner. This night I am driving Jeanie's car. As we pull into the driveway, the garage door rolls open and out comes a dark shape. He has been waiting patiently for us to come home. "Mr. Green Eyes" comes to greet us, eyes shining in the headlights, perhaps confused by night blindness.

I slow to a stop, then roll on a bit thinking, as always, that Wrangler is past the car.

There's a muffled thump, a yelp.

"Oh, no," I say to Jeanie. "I hope I didn't hit Wrangler."

I get out and go to the passenger side of the car and see Wrangler lying by the front tire.

I bend over him, cradle his head. "Here, boy, come here," I say, as he tries to pull free.

"Here, boy, let me see you. Come here."

He struggles to get up and seems to be dragging his right hip.

"I hope his leg isn't broken," I say. Jeanie says, "I think it's his hip."

He moves a couple of feet, lies down by our front steps.

"I have to get him to emergency care," I say. Jeanie suggests waiting until the morning to have him checked but I know I have to get help for him now.

It's cold and I am shivering. I race inside the house to get a jacket, call the nearest emergency vet service, get directions and tell them that I will be there in 15 minutes.

NINE YEARS WE WERE TOGETHER. IN NINE MINUTES WE WERE PARTED. NINE MINUTES...AN ERA WAS OVER, THE WRANGLER ERA OF MY LIFE.

Jeanie calls out, "Something is wrong with his breathing."

I run out. Wrangler has somehow pulled himself across the driveway to the far side and is very still, his pink tongue lolling to the side. A thin stream of blood spreads across the drive. He is not breathing.

I lean over, touch him gently, call his name, refusing what I fear most.

"My boy, my pal," I whisper. "I'm so sorry. I wouldn't have hurt you for anything. Wrangler, my boy, my pal."

He is not breathing. His eyes are open as they always were when he slept.

And I realize, Wrangler is gone — my Blue Heeler, my Aussie Cattle Dog, my pal of the last nine years.

I sprawl across his body on the cold pavement.

"What have I done? My doggie, my doggie, what have I done? Oh, Wrangler, I can't lose you. Please God, let him not die."

It is five weeks to the day since we had to put down our lovely cat, Butternut, nine years almost to the week from when I first found Wrangler, and he found me.

I wonder what he might have been thinking as he waited for us to come home? What was he expecting?

His Christmas gift, his jingle-bell doggies are on a shelf in the garage, waiting to sing "I Wish You a Merry Christmas."

All that remains is to take him to the vet, and days later to place his cremains on that same shelf until the time comes to scatter them.

Nine years we were together.

In nine minutes we were parted.

Nine minutes...an era was over, the Wrangler era of my life.

Wrangler was gone, the dog of my life.

A WAIL UNBIDDEN

A week later, a terrible wail comes unbidden from my lungs, a horror that rises and makes my whole body shake.

I see again that dark body lying on the cold cement — the body of the dog I love — eyes open, soft dark hair, a thin flow of blood from his mouth and a tiny stream of fluid behind. His eyes are open.

Silent. Gone.

Again that wail comes uncontrollably from deep inside me, like a cry from a scared child. It comes from the deepest darkness.

The way grief erupts is so unpredictable. It is like a full glass that needs only the slightest tip to overflow.

I go to church on Sunday but have to walk out.

It's hard to listen to Christmas music.

On my radio I hear a group singing a lovely old hymn, "In the sweet by and by, we shall meet on that beautiful shore," and I picture Wrangler running to me. The tears come.

I go by the Earth Fare store and see the railing where he often sat so patiently, waiting while I enjoyed a cool drink and sat reading on the patio.

In the sky I see two contrails from jets lit by the setting sun and think of the way the two of us walked together.

Where can I walk that Wrangler did not walk with me — down the street, to the library, to the water feature, in the schoolyard?

On a late-night stroll I call out, "Wrangli, Wrangli." Again. Again, as forlorn a calling as the night.

One night I find myself singing over and over the old song, "My Bonnie," now doggie:

My doggie lies over the ocean,
My doggie lies over the sea,
Oh bring back my doggie to me.

I think that in my dotage, I might sing that again and again.

ON CHRISTMAS EVE

"All is well, all is well,"
the boy soprano sang
with the St. Thomas Choir
on Christmas Eve.
It was pure, clear, angelic.

"All is well."

I visualized my Wrangler lying
breathless, bloodless, lifeless
on the cold driveway
and singing to him,
"All is well, my doggie pal,
all is well. Rest in peace."

And wanting him
to raise his fine head,
fix his steady brown eyes on mine
and breathe back, "All is well,"
not just for him, but for my own
forlorn heart.

GRIEF THAT WON'T LET GO

Days later I go for the first time to the schoolyard where he and I walked together hundreds of times. I visualize him across the field, totally absorbed in his sniffing, then looking to see where I am and when he spots me, racing across the field to be with me. And I realize he will not run to me again.

The trauma of memory will not let go. I have been told over and over that it was not my fault, that Wrangler clearly was confused and somehow got close to the car, perhaps confused by the car lights.

It's true; I knew he was getting older, but I still feel responsible. I was driving. The "if onlys" keep rolling around in my head. *If only* we had not gone to dinner. *If only* I had not been driving Jeanie's car and had come to my side of the garage. *If only* I had waited to be absolutely sure he was out of the way. *If only* he had not been wedged in such a tight space between the car and the shrubs.

If only...

If only he had not been so eager to greet us when we came home.

The "if onlys" play all kinds of mental tricks on me. My son-in-law says, "Don't think you went over him. He went under the car." I know that's true, and that my sense of being responsible is not entirely rational. I know that Wrangler was confused, and put himself in danger without knowing it.

The shock of how he died was awful. I have relived it many times. The ache he left behind is even more painful. It's not guilt that I feel so much as grief for a dead friend, of what was done and cannot be undone. That is the terrible reality that came to me that night, the message I sent to friends: "I have killed my doggie."

He was so loyal. I never wanted to hurt him. The times when I stepped on his paw or dropped something on him accidently, I felt so bad. But there was never a feeling like this.

A PRAYER FROM ONE GRIEVING

Lord, I hope I do not
exasperate you
with these grief moments
that come unsummoned,
when there is beauty
in the morning blaze,
laughter as a candle almost lights,
a robe at church,
friends who care so much.

Please be patient with me.
I am trying, practicing
as Mary Oliver says,
how to carry
him in my heart
until I can scatter
his ashes
in the wind.

ONE THREAD PULLS THEM ALL

It may sound morbid, this attachment. But grief has its way. It drains me. And the reservoir of regret empties itself a little more each time.

My friend, Jim, a counselor, suggests what I am missing. "He was always there, always available, always trusting, listening. I have known you as a leader who has always been 'one up.' I think you are just missing your friend. And with his loss you feel every other loss."

The loss that pulls at one thread pulls them all.

I cannot help thinking *Wrangli, I wish you — we — could have had one more spring, one more summer, one more fall.*

LENTEN LOSSES

The loss of Wrangler was very acute during Lent, because his loss also pulled other threads — friends very ill, spiritual companions who had died, a grandson surviving a terrible motorcycle accident, the terrible calamities and conflicts in the news every day.

And yet isn't this what Lent is about? We follow a Lord who endured a 40-day battle with the devil alone in the desert; who prayed in the garden all night with tears of blood and asked his disciples why they could not have stayed awake with him; who in his final moments cried out, "My God, why have you forsaken me?"

And yet, by his very sharing of our human condition, he reached out to us, taking unto himself the loneliness of our suffering, sin and separation, so that in turn he could offer his friendship and walk with us on our lonely roads.

So the questions that faced me this Lent were threefold: Would I let go of my losses? Would I reach out to receive (and to share) what God offers? How could I turn losses into new life?

Thinking back a decade to the time Wrangler and I met, I remember how the whole landscape, or "inscape," of life was changing in so many ways — a new ministry calling, old friends gone and making new ones, health challenges faced and overcome. It was a time of profound change of people, places, interests.

Looking back even further, I realized how much of life had emerged out of trauma — the leaving of my adopted parents; the loss of our son, Sandy, during heart surgery; the discovery of my birth parents when I was near 50; struggles and conflicts in ministry — as well as wonderful surprises that followed.

So, I wonder, out of the loss of my beloved Wrangler, what new will come? What gain from the loss? What will I discover about myself as God's beloved, my identity and calling?

What do my doggie and the Great Shepherd have to teach me about the fear of abandonment, the need to be adored, the longing for love that does not depend on being perfect?

EASTER TIME

Irish poet/philosopher John O'Donohue said, "It is such a waste to become absent from life."

Over these months I am moving on to life without Wrangler. It is slow. It is painful. But it is happening.

Easter weekend this year is a crucial moment in being present. On Good Friday I hear a message on the three prayers of Jesus on the cross — the prayer of abandonment ("My God, why...?"), the prayer of forgiveness ("Father, forgive them..."), the prayer of relinquishment ("Into your hands I commit my spirit.").

The next day I am driving to the "Y" for a workout and thinking of that message of abandonment, forgiveness, relinquishment. What does each mean to me?

When I come to "forgiveness," a huge welling of tears comes rushing from some closed place in me, more than the usual flow. Why?

And then the answer comes, one big reason I am finding it so hard to let go of him.

It's that I haven't forgiven myself for my part in Wrangler's end. Accidental as it was, I was still the one driving. And though he was aging, and though I am now spared the final act of ever having to put him down, I still feel a need for him to forgive me and a need to forgive myself.

"Wrangler," I breathe, "forgive me. I did not know what I was doing. If only I had paid better attention, stopped, made sure you were safely past the car."

I remember that last night bending over him and saying, "I am so sorry. I would never hurt you. I am so sorry."

Now I know that he understands, and so do I.

WE ARE NOT LEFT COMFORTLESS

"God does not leave us comfortless" wrote poet Jane Kenyon in "Let Evening Come."

As the weeks passed through winter into spring, God did not leave me comfortless. The "Comforter," his Spirit, reached out to me through many voices and hearts…a then eight-year-old girl, a poet, friends, another dog.

The eight-year-old was my granddaughter, Leighton.

We were at her house. She was showing me pictures on her iPhone and I told her I had some sad ones, photos of Wrangler at the end. She immediately understood.

She put her face against mine, patted me and said, "It's okay, Gagi. It's okay. You'll see him again. He's waiting for you. It's okay.

"He's watching over you. The Bible tells us people and animals watch over us when they die. He knows you love him." She would not stop until she was sure I was okay, for awhile at least.

Such wisdom, such comforting, at age eight.

Perhaps she is theologically correct. When God renewed his covenant with humankind after the great flood, he made it with all creatures, not just with humans. And in the new heaven and new earth to come all creatures will be present to praise him. (See Genesis 8:12-17 and Revelation 5:13-14.)

Yet, I still wonder why memories bring tears more than laughter? And how slowly will that change?

GAGI TEARS

Leighton was telling Jeanie that she had a pain in her jaw that was making her cry. Jeanie told her that she, too, had cried at times when she was hurting.

"Grownups don't cry," said Leighton.

"Yes they do," broke in sister Anabel. "You know Mom cries."

"Gagi does," said Jeanie. "You know that. You've seen him cry over Wrangler."

"But that's because he's another gender," Leighton retorted quite firmly.

"Another gender?" Jeanie was astonished. "What is that?"

"The Gagi gender," Leighton replied.

A POET

God reaches out to us through his human envoys like my granddaughter, an angel for my soul, and through poets such as Wendell Berry (WB).

These two — WB and WBD (Wrangler Blue Dog) — were almost coexistent in my life for nine years. On Sunday mornings, Wrangler and I would go to the woods, sit by the bridge, and while Wrangler sniffed some fascinating scent, I would select one of Berry's poems as a kind of devotional for the day and the week to come.

Wrangler would come and lie down beside me, and turn over to have his tummy rubbed while I read selected poems from Berry's "A Timbered Choir."

*I know that I have life
only insofar as I have love.*

*I have no love
except it come from Thee.*

*Help me, please, to carry
this candle against the wind.*

I read again from another collection of Berry's poems, "This Day: Collected and New Sabbath Poems, 1998."

*Whatever happens,
those who have learned
to love one another
have made their way
to the lasting world
and will not leave,
whatever happens.*

I found his words appropriate and comforting.

At the end, Wrangler and I did not go to the woods on Sunday mornings as often. But the last photos I have of the two of us are of my doggie and me walking in those woods, both gazing up first at each other, then at the sky, a visual memory of a devoted companion, who will not walk those woods, sniff those smells or lie peacefully on the bridges again. I imagine a bark from someplace not far away.

COMFORT OF FRIENDS

Friends have been comforters — Jim, who checked on me weekly for several months to see how I was doing; and Elizabeth, who first introduced me to Wrangler wrote in a message about a very clear dream in which she was at the Charlotte animal shelter, found Wrangler, and brought him to a young man. "I wanted to let you know how very all right he is," she said. "We can always walk with him in spirit here, and some day in the heavenly country."

A COMFORT DOG

And then there is Buddy, our new doggie.

Within days of Wrangler's departure, our daughter-in-law saw on a friend's Facebook a dog found wandering. She called and told her friend she wanted that dog. His microchip phone number and address led to no owner. So Buddy came to live with us, now a comfort dog.

Buddy is a Tibetan Terrier with two layers of thick blue-black hair. When he passes someone they almost always want to take him home. Where Wrangler was a one-person dog, Buddy is an all-persons dog, a connecting dog for us. When I get up in the morning he waits outside Jeanie's door until she gets up, then runs to tell me and joins the two of us in a group hug.

No dog can take the place of my lifetime dog. But Buddy is a comfort dog. For Jeanie, he helps fill the emptiness left by Butternut and Wrangler. They adore each other. When she gives him his good-night treat, he jumps two feet in the air, rolls over and around, and makes her laugh like a young girl.

Could it be that Wrangler (and his Great Master) had something to do with this new arrival?

Wrangler must still be my spiritual director, advising me to look to God and listen, much as Wrangler always looked to me.

LETTING GO, OPENING UP

"Love survives the death of cells."

Those words of a scientist-poet echo in my heart.

Wrangler and I loved each other in life, and I love him in his death.

Of course, there is always risk in loving any creature. If we love deeply we face the certainty of hurting deeply, for love and loss do connect.

And I realize now that Wrangler has been my teacher in making that connection.

- He taught me with his daily doggie routines to *live* simply.
- With his unwavering gaze he taught me to *love* attentively.
- Now he is teaching me to *let go*, gratefully and openly.

There is an ancient understanding of spiritual life known as kenosis, or self-emptying. It comes directly from the Bible, shown fully in Christ who "emptied himself" even to the death of the cross, taking on himself our sins and our pains to bring us fullness of life. Kenosis is not just about losing. It is about emptying ourselves so we can be open to receive what gifts yet will come to us on our journey.

If Wrangler was my "spiritual director dog" then he may also have been a pointer, now pointing me to let go, to open up from loss, to stop resisting and to receive, to breathe fresh new air.

Among other things, the older I get I need to remind myself to be more careful. As my physical abilities diminish, I need to be more alert to danger and to care for physical needs and limitations.

More important is to pay attention to the Lord, as Wrangler paid attention to me, his eyes fixed, watching for any sign to which he could respond. And, in particular, to remember how important it is just to "be with" the one you love.

STILL, A CONFESSION

I confess, as is more than obvious, that I have had a very hard time letting Wrangler go. He is absent and, at the same time, very much with me. I see him everywhere. I still find it difficult to walk where we spent time together — walking among the periwinkles in the spring, dancing in the water in summertime, joining the prayer circle at retreats with youth leaders in the fall.

The blue collar he wore his last few years hangs on my bedpost. I will leave it there, perhaps as long as I have that bed. I loved him as no other creature apart from my family. It is difficult for me to describe the love we had for each other. We were content just to be together.

I think of him now, the touch of his body, his soft hair, the gray streak on his head.

His crate has been folded and put away. His blue dish, the rim cracked, is on a shelf in the garage as is the plaque "Australian Cattle Dog." But the blue collar I keep close. I miss him.

There was a time recently during a retreat in the North Carolina mountains when we were asked to step

> **MY LIFETIME DOGGIE WILL HAVE HIS PLACE IN THE SOIL AND THE SUN AND THE WIND — MOST OF ALL IN MY HEART AND MEMORY FOR MY LIFETIME. BUT TIME WILL PASS, AND HEALING WILL COME.**

outside and listen for what resonated most in our minds and hearts. And this is what I heard: Stop resisting. Be open to receiving.

Wrangler's ashes are safely stored next to those of his nemesis, Butternut. I have already begun to spread some of his ashes in various special places.

My lifetime doggie will have his place in the soil and the sun and the wind — most of all in my heart and memory for my lifetime. But time will pass, and healing will come.

In words from "The Great Storm is Over," sung by John McCutcheon, "Lift up your wings and fly!"

It is over…almost. Wrangler is flying.

And I believe I am ready to take up my wings. This is more than wishful thinking, or a philosophical acceptance that all good things come to an end.

It is a true and strong hope. Jesus' relinquishment was not the end. Resurrection followed the cross — a resurrection not only for him but for all of us, and for all creation.

The great storm will be over because the great victory has been won.

VISION OF HOPE

Jeanie and I had been to Montreat to visit her brother, Billy.

It was so poignant to see him as an old man, sitting slumped in his chair, a baseball cap pulled over his eyes, recognizing us with difficulty.

"It's okay for you to move to heaven," Jeanie said to him gently.

Coming back down the mountain we were quiet. "When do you miss Wrangler most?" she asked.

"Late afternoon," I said. "About now, when I would come home and he was waiting to take a walk."

I turned on the radio and suddenly the car was filled with a magnificent choir singing "The Hallelujah Chorus."

Then it was as if I had — what? — a vision, an image, as if Wrangler was being lifted, almost levitated to another world.

He was standing in the Holy City with a great crowd. His tail was up, his ears raised, his head cocked in his usual pose of alert, his lovely head lifted to the light at the center — and he was singing.

Wrangler had a bark that was totally singular. We always could recognize the tones, one when he heard me coming home, another when a delivery truck went by.

In that great chorus coming through the radio his ACD bark was totally his own, yet blended with all the others.

"Forever and ever…forever…forever."

And why not?

If there is to be a new heaven and a new earth, if heaven is not a fairyland beyond the sky but heaven and earth remade; if there is another world that is

> THAT RICH GLOW IN THE SKY IS MY PROMISE THAT ANOTHER DAY WILL COME, ANOTHER GATE WILL OPEN. AND THEN WE WILL WALK THROUGH TOGETHER. THEN. NOW. AND FOREVER.

also invisibly within this present one; if the kingdom of God is within us; then Wrangler may even now be singing the song of all creatures as in the great throng of Revelation.

After we arrived home, I walked out into the darkening streets.

Where could I walk that Wrangler had not walked with me — down the street, to the library, to the supermarket, to the water feature, the schoolyard.

I couldn't move. I was truly frozen. There was no place for me to go without remembering him.

Then I remembered the prayer I prayed to the Great Shepherd the morning after Wrangler died. "Come with me," I whispered, "and I will go into the schoolyard where my doggie and I walked hundreds of times."

Then I could see him, a dark figure at the iron gate — and his little habits, turning to the right at the gate to sniff, going through the gate and turning to the left, sniffing again, then ready to walk.

Across the far sky beyond the houses and trees I could see day's end, a long wide red ribbon of light, stretching it seemed for miles, above it dark blue, lighter beneath, almost like a huge horizontal rainbow.

I could hear in my soul God's voice, saying, "It's okay. The time will come. The light of day may be going now. But that rich glow in the sky is my promise that another day will come, another gate will open. And then we will walk through together."

Then. Now. And forever.

A POSTSCRIPT

Wrangler's ashes had been scattered in several special places…by the lake, on a fairway at Grandfather Golf and Country Club, on a curve in the mountains above Banner Elk.

There was one place I had not been able to walk since Wrangler died — the water park near our home. It had been so sacred, so special, and memories were painful.

I wanted to put ashes there but not until my young friend, Nick, could join me, who over half a dozen years had walked there with Wrangler and me many times.

On a hot afternoon, with Buddy ambling along, Nick and I walked along the creek to the bridge where on Sundays I so often sat and read.

While Buddy looked around, Nick and I sat and I again read from Wendell Berry's "A Timbered Choir," the margin of which noted that I had read the same poem on this bridge on November 20, 2005, not quite a year after Wrangler came to me.

It was fitting, as Berry's words in that poem reminded me, that Wrangler, like all God's creatures, had found his contentment to be what God made him.

That was his pleasure, and mine.

With a trowel, Nick and I opened a small place near the bridge and placed there a container of Wrangler's ashes. I prayed a brief prayer of thanks, covered the place with earth and needles, and a stone Nick found nearby. I laid my hand on the stone, "My doggie, my pal."

We scattered a few more ashes to float on the stream, some along a low wall, some in a bed of grasses and flowers, and walked silently away.

"What was Wrangler's greatest gift to you?" asked Nick.

"His presence," I said immediately. "One of the first commands I taught him, and that he taught me, was simply 'with me.'"

And he was — with me, and I with him.

WRANGLER'S DREAM

This abstract painting is based on a friend's photograph of the water feature in Morrocroft where Wrangler and I posed for family pictures. It reminds me of the times I walked here with Wrangler and his stops at the creek for a drink. Perhaps the maelstrom reflects the churning of my emotions that surged when Wrangler left only days later. Perhaps it reflects what this scene looked like to a dog pausing to drink. Perhaps, above all, it speaks to the mysterious bond which connects a dog and his mister, a connection which perhaps no one else can quite see, feel or understand. Or, perhaps this might be the flow of colors and shapes which Wrangler saw that day in the woods — and perhaps in his final sleep. I would like to think so.

Leighton S. Ford

ACKNOWLEDGMENTS

My faithful doggie friend, Wrangler, is in my heart and memory always. He and I shared a very special journey. For the "love of friends" who were part of that journey, gratitude and thanks to...

- Kind caretakers at Charlotte Mecklenburg Animal Care and Control in Charlotte, North Carolina, who rescued Wrangler and kept him safe.
- Elizabeth, a friend, who discerned the right dog for the right person and brought Wrangler into my life.
- Young Ben, who helped me choose Wrangler.
- My wife, Jean, who opened our home and her heart to Wrangler.
- Butternut, also known as Sir B, the cat who often made life interesting.
- Nick, who shared many walks.
- Sally, who guided me in painting illustrations of Wrangler and Butternut.
- Veterinarians and assistants at Sharon Lakes Animal Hospital in Charlotte for their expert care of Wrangler.

A special word of thanks to Paul Harmel, chairman and CEO of *Lifetouch • Photography for a Lifetime*, and all those who worked to produce this book. His talented team took great care to assemble the poems, paintings, photographs and words into this story about Wrangler, one that I treasure and share with joy.

Leighton S. Ford
Charlotte, North Carolina

LEIGHTON FORD

Leighton Ford is widely known as a preacher, speaker and author, having spoken to large crowds in 40 countries. Ordained as an evangelist by the Presbyterian Church, he describes evangelism as "making friends for God."

In recent years he has focused on mentoring emerging younger leaders around the world, helping them, as he says, to "lead more like Jesus and more to Jesus."

What is not as well known, except to his friends, is that he is also an artist and poet.

"God is an artist," he says. "He has painted this world and his creatures — like Wrangler and Butternut — with beauty. We have a responsibility both to enjoy and care for his creation."

A native of Canada, as a teenager Leighton met Billy Graham, who encouraged him to attend Wheaton College in Illinois, where he studied philosophy and, more importantly, met his future wife, Billy's sister Jean. They were married while he did his theological studies at Columbia Theological Seminary in Georgia. Following graduation, he worked for some years with Billy Graham before launching Leighton Ford Ministries.

Leighton and Jean live in Charlotte, North Carolina, near to their daughter, Debbie, and son Kevin, their spouses, and five grandchildren and two great-grandchildren. Their beloved son, Sandy, died during heart surgery when he was 21.

Asked whether his mission has changed from his years as an evangelist, Leighton smiles. "No. He has called me to be an artist of the soul and a friend on the journey."

Leighton's latest book is *The Attentive Life*. He is currently writing a memoir about his calling. To learn more about Leighton's ministry, and his paintings and writings, please visit *LeightonFordMinistries.org/Gallery*.

Lifetouch Image